IMAGES
of America

MACKINAC BRIDGE

The Bridge at Mackinac
by Dr. David B. Steinman

In the land of Hiawatha,
Where the white man gazed with awe
At a paradise divided
By the Straits of Mackinac

Men are dredging, drilling, blasting,
Battling tides around the clock,
Through the depths of icy water,
Driving caissons down to rock.

Fleets of freighters bring their cargoes
From the forges and the kilns;
Stones and steel - ten thousand barge-loads -
From the quarries, mines, and mills.

Now the towers, mounting skyward,
Reach the heights of airy space.
Hear the rivet-hammers ringing,
Joining steel in strength and grace.

High above the swirling currents,
Parabolic strands are strung;
From the cables, packed with power,
Wonder-spans of steel are hung.

Generations dreamed the crossing;
Doubters shook their heads in scorn.
Brave men vowed that they would build it -
From their faith a bridge was born.

There it spans the miles of water,
Speeding millions on their way -
Bridge of vision, hope and courage,
Portal to a brighter day.

Dr. David B. Steinman, engineer and the designer of the Mackinac Bridge, wrote this poem titled *The Bridge at Mackinac* as one of his many works about the span.

On the cover: The cover photograph, graciously shared by Ken Teysen, of Teysen's Gallery in Mackinaw City, shows visitors gathered on the Mackinaw City shoreline to watch the bridge take shape. Missing sections made the bridge appear as a mirage until the link was completed between Michigan's two peninsulas.

IMAGES
of America

MACKINAC BRIDGE

Mike Fornes

ARCADIA
PUBLISHING

Published by Arcadia Publishing
Charleston, South Carolina

Library of Congress Catalog Card Number: 2007924800

For all general information contact Arcadia Publishing at:
Telephone 843-853-2070
Fax 843-853-0044
E-mail sales@arcadiapublishing.com
For customer service and orders:
Toll-Free 1-888-313-2665

Visit us on the Internet at www.arcadiapublishing.com

*This book is dedicated to the memory of Dr. David B. Steinman,
engineer, author, and poet.*

CONTENTS

ACKNOWLEDGMENTS

Gathering the many photographs and stories of the Mackinac Bridge would have been a much more laborious task without the help of Susan Godzik and the resources of the wonderful Michigan Room at the Mackinaw Area Public Library. Mackinaw City is indeed fortunate to have such a wealth of information about the Mackinac Bridge, the Straits Area, and the state of Michigan in one annex. To the library and staff, I am deeply indebted.

The bridge's stories have been told over the years by leading newspapers of the state, and my grateful thanks go to the *Detroit News*, *Detroit Free Press*, *Grand Rapids Press*, *Lansing State Journal*, *Sault Evening News*, *St. Ignace News*, *Petoskey News-Review* and fellow staffers and coworkers at my own *Cheboygan Daily Tribune* for their assistance, courtesies, and access to archived information.

The Mackinac Bridge Authority's present-day staff, especially Bob Sweeney, Dean Steiner, and Lorraine Garries, is thanked for their willingness to help chase down dates and recall memories and circumstances. Past administrator Walter North took a special interest in helping me organize people, places, and topics in the bridge's history. In addition, many local law enforcement personnel helped in significant ways.

When it came to getting the facts right, I was lucky to have a resource nearby like Dick Campbell, who worked on the bridge as a diver, painter, maintenance man, and so much more during his years of employment there.

The Michigan Department of Transportation is deserving of special thanks for its generosity in accessing archival photographs from a meticulously organized and maintained database. Unless specified otherwise, the photographs used in this publication were provided to me by the Michigan Department of Transportation's Photograph Section.

Other quality photographs were obtained through the helpfulness of the Mackinaw Area Visitors Bureau and the Mackinaw City Chamber of Commerce.

Finally, there could have been no better ultimate source for detail than Larry Rubin, past executive secretary of the Mackinac Bridge Authority.

It is my hope that those who read this work will better appreciate all that went into past crossings, and further marvel at David B. Steinman's genius during their next trip across. His genius as a bridge builder united the state of Michigan in a way that few thought possible in the 1950s and before. His writings about bridge architecture are legendary in that his understated style continues to serve as the template for engineers world-wide. His poetry reveals a man with a deep spirit who could write, "A poem in steel, a dream-span in bedrock, a symphony in metal and stone. The mystical union of beauty and strength. A lyric pattern etched against the blue. God working through man to confute the powers of evil and to add another stanza to the hymn of creation." David B. Steinman indeed created "a bridge built by faith."

INTRODUCTION

Since opening to traffic in 1957, the Mackinac Bridge has seen much more than the millions of vehicles that have crossed the five-mile span. America's longest suspension bridge has withstood gale-force winds, the pressure of crushing ice floes, and blinding snowstorms. It has been repeatedly struck by lightning and hit by an airplane and a ship—yet still stands as perhaps the safest five miles of Interstate 75.

Expertly maintained by a close-knit crew that paints, plows, and patrols its four lanes on a year-round basis, the Mackinac Bridge, or "Mighty Mac," united Michigan's two peninsulas and still serves as the sole highway link across an open-water strait that is 300 feet deep. Parades of vehicles and pedestrians have crossed over the Mackinac Bridge and flotillas of ships have passed under it. This engineering wonder is indeed a symbol of the state of Michigan. But the process of getting the bridge built began long before the first foundations were set in the Straits of Mackinac.

Years ago, there was no shortage of plans for linking Michigan's two peninsulas. A floating tunnel was suggested in 1920 by Horatio Earle, Michigan's first state highway commissioner. Another proposal suggested building a series of causeways and bridges from Cheboygan to Bois Blanc Island to Round Island, across the western tip of Mackinac Island and then across to St. Ignace. Each plan failed because financial and physical problems seemed insurmountable.

In 1934, Murray D. Van Wagoner, then Democratic state highway commissioner, insisted that the Michigan legislature create a Mackinac Straits Bridge Authority to study the feasibility of a bridge; in 1940, the Mackinac Straits Bridge Authority reported to the legislature that a bridge at the straits was feasible. One year later, Van Wagoner became governor and during his administration a million-dollar causeway was built at the northern approach to the projected bridge, reaching one-mile south into the straits from St. Ignace.

Van Wagoner was defeated in 1942, and no further action was taken. The United States had, by this time, entered into World War II. There was not enough money, workers, or materials available to build a bridge because everything was being put into the war effort.

In 1947, the war over, the legislature terminated the Mackinac Straits Bridge Authority. G. Mennen Williams, a young U.S. Navy veteran, was nominated on the Democratic ticket for governor despite having never before run for elective office. Williams promised to revive the Mackinac Bridge project if elected. He won the governor's office in November 1948.

In 1949, Williams appointed the Inter-Peninsula Communications Commission to study the bridge question and other problems arising out of the separation of the two peninsulas. The Inter-Peninsula Communications Commission, headed by John McCarthy, head of the Michigan Public Service Commission, brought the bridge studies out of the Michigan State Highway Department files and reported that the bridge was feasible.

Governor Williams recommended in 1950 that a Mackinac Bridge Authority be reestablished, with power to build a bridge. Democrats and Republicans in the legislature joined to reestablish the Mackinac Bridge Authority, but denied it the power to go beyond studying the question. Members of the authority were appointed by Governor Williams, who retained three engineers to study the project. In 1951, the Mackinac Bridge Authority reported to the legislature that a bridge at the straits was feasible from all standpoints—engineering, financial, and economic. Governor Williams again recommended in 1952 that the Mackinac Bridge Authority be empowered to act, and the legislature passed a bill specifying that the bridge must be financed by revenue bonds without cost to the state and without incurring any public indebtedness.

Dr. David B. Steinman, 63, was named as consulting engineer for the Mackinac project in 1953, and Glenn B. Woodruff was named as associate consultant. Also in 1953, Governor Williams, Sen. Prentiss M. Brown, and members of the Mackinac Bridge Authority met in New York City with a group of investment bankers. Governor Williams told the bankers that the bridge would provide "a new Northwest Passage" and that "the great Atlantic East will be joined with the wheat and oil fields of Canada."

The bankers were impressed, but the bond market was "soft." Economic conditions were not ripe for a bond issue of nearly $100 million. On the advice of the bond counsel, the Mackinac Bridge Authority asked the legislature to demonstrate the good faith of the state by paying the annual maintenance cost of the bridge out of state highway funds. The legislature agreed that $417,000 per year be diverted from highway funds for bridge maintenance, on the condition that the bonds be sold by December 31, 1953.

With this assurance of state support, the sale of the bonds was arranged by mid-December. However, the bridge was almost stopped when Michigan senator Haskell L. Nichols, a Republican from Jackson who had voted against the bridge, filed a lawsuit in the Michigan Supreme Court asking for an injunction to prevent approval of the bond sale by the state administrative board. The lawsuit was filed 24 hours before the scheduled sale of the bonds. Had this move succeeded, the $417,000 appropriation would have lapsed and the bridge would have been set back at least a year, and possibly for many years. The court refused the injunction, and later, after a hearing, upheld the state administrative board's approval of the bridge's financing.

Groundbreaking ceremonies were held in St. Ignace on May 7, 1954, and in Mackinaw City on May 8. Large crowds attended the festivities on both sides of the bridge.

Construction began immediately, and although the work on the water shut down each winter, it continued on the mainland with crews readying bridge sections that were brought out by barge in the spring and summer to be lifted into place. The bridge was completed on time, on budget, and with private financing.

The ferryboats were charging an average of $3.40 per car and passengers when the boats stopped running on November 1, 1957.

One

MICHIGAN, A STATE DIVIDED

Before the Mackinac Bridge was opened in 1957, the Michigan Department of Transportation operated a ferry system between Mackinaw City and St. Ignace that took passengers and vehicles across the Straits of Mackinac. This five-mile stretch of turbulent water divided Michigan's two peninsulas, creating a physical, legislative, and many times economic barrier. Though passengers then knew no other way, they could not have predicted how a bridge would impact the lives of those making the crossing. For some, the boat trip was an annual event to be endured over a period of 24 hours, for lines backed up as much as 20 miles in either direction. Today citizens of Mackinaw City or St. Ignace sometimes use the bridge to commute to work, to school, or for recreation and use the bridge each day and sometimes have several crossings in a single day. Traffic lineups mostly occurred during holiday periods such as Memorial Day, the week surrounding the Fourth of July holiday, Labor Day weekend, and sometimes the entire month of August. Severe storms could also back up traffic until the boats began moving once again.

But no time of the year summarized the frustration of motorists crossing the straits more than during firearm deer hunting season. During the last deer season before the bridge, November 1956, there was a 23-mile lineup of cars coming north that stretched 15 miles on Old U.S. Route 27 and 8 miles on U.S. Route 31. Service stations were equipped with hoses to the gas pumps that were as long as 100 feet so that cars could be fueled while remaining in line as they passed the station. Besides the threat of running out of gas, filling the tank on the Lower Peninsula side was important because gasoline was considerably more expensive in the Upper Peninsula in those days. The same trips take place today but cross the Straits of Mackinac via the bridge that allows the same passage in less than 10 minutes. The "Miracle Bridge at Mackinac" signifies joy and wonder to many, a landmark of the beginning of a great journey or perhaps a destination in itself.

Until 1954, shorelines at the Straits of Mackinac were beaches where the roadways ended, north and south. This stretch, at Mackinaw City on the south shore, was a state park where campers gazed in awe upon the seemingly impassable stretch of five miles of open water. A ferryboat was the only way for passengers, railroad cars, and automobiles to cross it.

Waiting lines for ferryboats at the straits were commonplace beginning in the 1930s and got progressively worse in the 1940s and 1950s, leading up to the construction of the bridge. Although the average wait could be as little as two hours most of the time, peak travel weekends such as Memorial Day, Labor Day, and the Fourth of July were overshadowed by the entire month of August and firearm deer hunting season in November. Waiting times then could be as much as 24 hours with traffic inching along almost constantly along U.S. Route 31 and M 27 from the south, and U.S. Route 2 from the north. Gasoline stations along the route had hoses of 100 feet in length to fuel cars directly from the pumps to the roadway, so motorists would not lose their place in line.

The State of Michigan continually added to its fleet of ferryboats but still could not handle the peak traffic periods. The ferry *City of Petoskey* (shown at the Mackinaw City dock) was typical of boats that had been converted from train ferries for automobile use. A lineup such as this on the state docks alone would represent a waiting time of four to five hours, even though the boats ran continuously. The state's largest and most modern ferry, *Vacationland*, could load or unload from either end and could be piloted from either end of the vessel. After the bridge was completed, many ferryboat workers became employed working for the Mackinac Bridge Authority. *Vacationland* was eventually sold for scrap and was being towed to China when it encountered a storm on the Pacific Ocean and sank in water nearly two miles deep.

Prentiss M. Brown is considered to be the "Father of the Mackinac Bridge." A former U.S. senator, his political connections paved the way for putting together a plan and the backing necessary to build the link across the Straits of Mackinac. Brown's key allies in the project were Michigan governor G. Mennen Williams and financial catalyst Charles T. Fisher Jr. In addition, Brown found vital local support for the bridge in W. Stewart Woodfill, owner and operator of Mackinac Island's Grand Hotel. Woodfill was committed to the idea of a bridge to promote tourism and travel to Michigan's Upper Peninsula. Brown served as the chairman of the Mackinac Bridge Authority from 1950 to 1973. He used to say that it cost him $16 to ship his Model T Ford across the straits in a car ferry. Many important businessmen were delayed during winter crossings, when ferries often got stuck in the ice despite their ice breaking capabilities. Brown resolved to end that chapter in the straits's transportation story.

the *Mackinac* bridge

Interesting Facts

Length of Main Span...................................... 3,800 Ft.

Length of Suspension Bridge (Including Anchorages).... 8,614 Ft.

Total Length of Steel Superstructure....................17,918 Ft.

Length of North Approach (Including Mole)............ 7,791 Ft.

Length of South Approach........................... 486 Ft.

Total Length of Bridge and Approaches................26,195 Ft.

Height of Main Towers Above Water................... 552 Ft.

Depth of Tower Piers Below Water.................... 200 Ft.

Number of Main Cables.............................. 2

Diameter of Main Cables............................ 24¼ Inches

Number of Wires in Each Cable......................12,876

Diameter of each Wire.............................. 0.196 Inches

Total Length of Cable Wire.........................41,000 Miles

Weight of Cable, Wire and Fittings..................12,500 Tons

Total Estimated Weight of Superstructure..............66,000 Tons

The Mackinac Bridge was heralded in engineering journals, tourist trade publications, and travel magazines as the longest suspension bridge in the world as it neared completion in 1957. Besides its incredible length, the statistics boasted record numbers in the amount of cable wire and rivets used and sheer volumes of concrete and steel. Although the center-span area of the Mackinac Bridge is shorter than some other notable bridges, the total suspended structure of the bridge surpasses those that rivaled it before or immediately after it was built. To achieve these numbers, it was necessary to combine several different construction techniques. Some processes were established in past efforts and many were new, but the uniqueness of the project was established when all were married together in one massive project. These standards stood for more than 40 years until bridges on other continents eventually eclipsed the Mackinac Bridge's record-setting statistics.

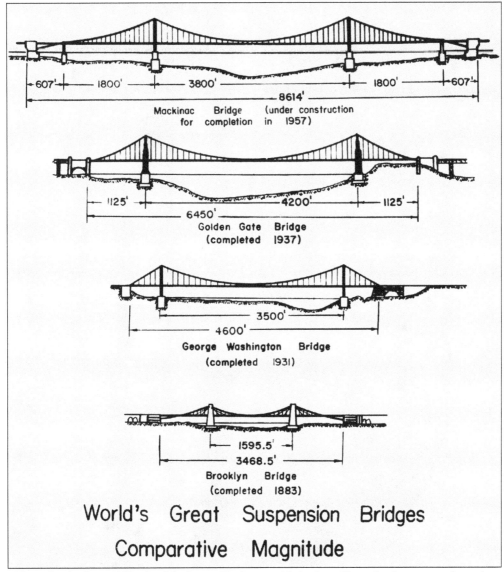

| ← 607' → | ← 1800' → | ← 3800' → | ← 1800' → | ← 607' → |

8614'

Mackinac Bridge (under construction for completion in 1957)

| ← 1125' → | ← 4200' → | ← 1125' → |

6450'

Golden Gate Bridge
(completed 1937)

3500'

4600'

George Washington Bridge
(completed 1931)

1595.5'

3468.5'

Brooklyn Bridge
(completed 1883)

World's Great Suspension Bridges
Comparative Magnitude

When finished in 1957, the Mackinac Bridge established itself as the longest and costliest suspension bridge in the world, surpassing San Francisco's Golden Gate Bridge. Since the Mackinac Bridge was built, two bridges have been completed that have longer total suspended spans, pushing the Mackinac Bridge to third on the worldwide list. In second place is Denmark's Great Belt Bridge that is the suspension bridge in a series of connections between the Danish islands of Zealand and Funen across the Great Belt of Denmark. The Akashi-Kaikyo Bridge, also known as the Pearl Bridge, is a suspension bridge in Japan that crosses the Akashi Strait; it links Maiko in Kobe and Iwaya on Awaji Island as part of the Honshu-Shikoku Highway. As of 2007, it ranked as the longest suspension bridge in the world. Compared to Mackinac Bridge's 8,614 feet of total suspended span, the Great Belt Bridge stretches to 8,921 feet, and the Akashi-Kaikyo has a whopping 12,831 feet of suspended span.

MUD

BEDROCK

This artist's conceptual view of the massive project of building the bridge's foundations and superstructure is accurate in displaying the enormous amount of work that had to be undertaken below the surface of the Straits of Mackinac. Invisible to the eyes of passengers crossing above, approximately two-thirds of the bridge's superstructure is underwater. Several theories popular in the 1920s and 1930s had dissuaded attempts to build a bridge, including the supposed presence of underwater caverns below the lake bottom that would prevent caissons from being anchored in solid bedrock. In reality, modern engineering overcame the tremendous distance across the straits—five miles—over the deep channel through the center of a chasm that is nearly 300 feet deep. Each tower stands in 210 feet of water—an unconscionable depth for marine construction of this magnitude in the mid-1900s. The challenges were overcome due to the genius of the man selected to design the new bridge, Dr. David B. Steinman.

Two

THE ENGINEERING
GENIUS

Any crossing of the Mackinac Bridge, or a look from various angles surrounding it, inspires awe at the building of such a magnificent structure. Now imagine designing a bridge of this magnitude in the 1950s, and a real admiration for Dr. David B. Steinman results.

Steinman was born on June 11, 1886, in New York City. His parents, Eve and Louis Steinman, raised David and his six siblings in a small apartment near the Brooklyn Bridge. His early life was very different from the lives of other families in the neighborhood, many of them immigrant factory workers. Young Steinman took comfort and pride in education. He was first introduced to school at the age of five when his older sister took him to her principal so he could show off his mathematical genius. According to the principal, "He could rattle off powers of two: 2, 4, 6, 8, 16, and 32, up to a million." Teachers would often reward Steinman with candy when he would calculate answers to problems like 17 times 52 and 47 times 13. A box of candy was so treasured by the family that it would be nursed for three weeks, being kept on the fire escape because the Steinman apartment had no icebox.

Steinman attended college at the City College of New York, because he could not afford a private college and took some classes while still in high school. He paid his own way and graduated summa cum laude in 1906 with a bachelor of science degree. He obtained his engineering degree from Columbia University, along with two other degrees in 1909 with the help of fellowships, scholarships, and nighttime jobs.

In 1910, Steinman accepted an offer from the University of Idaho, and became the youngest civil engineering professor in America. His work over the next 40 years established him as one of the premiere bridge design engineers in the world.

In 1952, Steinman agreed to undertake the job of designing a suspension bridge across the Straits of Mackinac on speculation, connecting the Upper and Lower Peninsulas of Michigan, because the Michigan state government did not have funds to contract an engineer to do preliminary designs. When completed, Steinman called the bridge, "my crowning achievement—the consummation of a lifetime dedicated to my chosen profession of bridge engineering."

During a study of prospective Mackinac Bridge engineers, the Mackinac Bridge Authority posed a question to candidates, asking, "Gentlemen, what would happen to one of your foundations if a boat loaded with ore crashed into it?" One of those being interviewed, Dr. David B. Steinman, answered, "The boat would sink with a serious loss of life."

Steinman got the job over Orhmar H. Amman, a Swedish-born New Yorker, and Glenn B. Woodruff of San Francisco. Amman had built the George Washington and Whitestone Bridges in New York and many others throughout the country, and Woodruff had participated in the design of several structures in California including the Oakland Bay Bridge.

Steinman grew up selling newspapers in the shadow of the Brooklyn Bridge and told fellow newsboys that, "Someday I was going to build bridges like the famous structure that towered above us. They laughed at me." Years later, it was apparent that Steinman knew how to build bridges—his firm had been involved in the building of more than 400 bridges on five continents throughout the world.

A veritable genius who attended Columbia University, Steinman earned his doctorate degree in engineering at age 19 and was awarded honorary doctoral degrees from 22 different universities. A quotable man who spoke with an exacting, authoritative tone, Steinman stood barely five feet tall. He wrote poetry about his crown jewel, the Mackinac Bridge.

David Steinman's experience with other large bridge projects prompted him to encourage private financing for the Mackinac Bridge. The bridge was financed through a unique bond sale that covered its $100 million cost without using state or public funding. A certified cashier's check for $96,400,033.33 paid for the bridge, with the difference going to the hundreds of firms all over the United States who handled distribution of the bonds.

The bonds sold to pay for the Mackinac Bridge were retired July 1, 1986. In comparison, the Golden Gate Bridge only cost $36 million to build in 1937. The Mackinac Bridge was a far tougher sell in a "soft" bond market, plus the bridge was 300 miles from a major city. Investors worried if anyone would cross it and pay tolls to offset the bond costs.

Although Steinman did not engineer the Golden Gate Bridge project, he knew that he faced challenges far different from those seen in San Francisco Bay. In the Mackinac Straits, the winds and waves would be worse, the suspended span longer, and the water would freeze into ice that could be 10 feet thick during build-ups that would threaten to sweep clear anything left on the surface.

Steinman designed bridge foundations to support the superstructure and any live load it would carry by a safety factor of four. The steel superstructure, in turn, would withstand wind pressure of 50 pounds per square foot or wind velocities up to 600 miles per hour. In the 1950s, the highest wind velocity recorded to date at the Mackinac Straits was 78 miles per hour.

David Steinman and his wife, Irene, were guests of honor in the Dedication Festival Parade held June 28, 1958, the summer after the bridge opened to traffic. Steinman was a poet and an author in addition to being a master bridge engineer. He called the Mackinac Bridge "a bridge built by faith."

Prentiss M. Brown poses with Irene Steinman in 1961 after her husband's death. A plaque was dedicated in Dr. David B. Steinman's honor at St. Ignace, the site of his most prodigious project, the Mackinac Bridge. Among his other literary works, David wrote a book about his favorite bridge titled *Miracle Bridge at Mackinac.*

Three

ANCHORING THE MIGHTY MACKINAC BRIDGE

To anchor the 100 million gross tons of the Mackinac Bridge, man-made mountains were required to be built in 88 feet of water. Steel, concrete, and stone comprised the giant foundations that would hold 42,000 miles of cable stretched over twin towers 552 feet above the waterline. As the first structures of the bridge to be built, much attention was paid to the initial signs of progress on the wide-open Straits of Mackinac. Although the improvements were slow and the bulky formation seemed unlikely to be part of the bridge's sleek design, indeed the finished anchor piers solidified any concerns about the span's mammoth strength. The anchor blocks—piers 17 and 22—were to become the beginning and the end of the world's longest suspended span to date. Much was tied to the success of the huge square toeholds grown into the bedrock at the bottom of the lake.

The first signs of life in the Mackinac Bridge project appeared just before ground was officially broken, on May 7, 1954, in St. Ignace and on May 8 in Mackinaw City. Seven surveyor's towers served as the mainland points of reference for determining locations of all 34 pier locations. They remained until well into the construction process.

This triangular surveyor's tower, the eventual location of the south anchor block, pier 17, was one of six that were anchored in the straits, three on each side of the proposed center line of the bridge. By sighting along lines from one location to another, locations of each pier were placed exactly where engineers wanted them to be.

The harbor at St. Ignace became the home base for Merritt-Chapman and Scott's marine construction equipment, regarded in 1954 as the largest gathering of its type ever assembled for a civilian project. The bay offered weather protection and deep water for vessels involved in the project. Other operations were also based at Mackinaw City.

St. Ignace was the location for the land-based construction of the giant steel foundations and bridge support pieces. Each was a project bigger than had ever before been seen in St. Ignace. The ironworkers brought a different culture to town and their way of life changed the business climate in the area. Many workers liked the region and some decided to stay after the bridge was completed.

A bridge foundation section measuring 135 feet long, 35 feet wide, and 75 feet high is towed from St. Ignace out into the straits as part of preliminary construction in 1954. The work was weather-dependent, and crews waited for a chance to transport the giant forms to their permanent homes. The journeys were tenuous, at best, for sudden winds could make the trip and the placement a dangerous proposition.

Once the framework arrived at its destination, cranes lifted it off the barge and placed it on the lake bottom into a precise position within one-tenth of an inch. The frames were then tied to rock with spud piles. Two more sections followed to be placed on top of the first one to complete the formation of the giant anchor piers, one to each end of the suspension length.

Hard-hat divers were involved in the exact placement of the bridge framework and in subsequent inspection duty for piers and caissons. They relayed information to bridge foremen topside. The cumbersome dive suits of that era had a heavy brass helmet, leather fittings, and lead shoes. The divers were supplied with air from a surface compressor. The work was cold, dangerous, and tiring. Very little motion that resembled swimming took place, unlike conditions with modern, lightweight gear that is much safer. A bridge diver was the first of the five fatalities that took place during the three years of construction at the bridge. Decompression sickness, or "the bends," was a constant threat to the safety of the divers who worked in the extremely cold, deep water of the straits. (Courtesy of Richard Campbell)

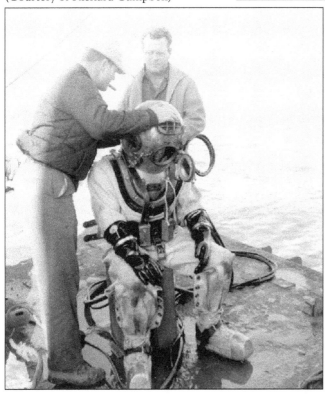

To fill the frameworks, cofferdams were built to hold specially-treated crushed stone brought by ship from Drummond Island, 50 miles away. The stone had to be of specific size, hardness, and cleanliness to meet the contractors' specifications. It was quarried, crushed, and washed several times to remove fine dust particles before being transported to the work site. There, a self-unloading freighter transferred the aggregates to the cofferdams. The job took three to four hours to unload 12,000 tons of stone. It then had to be repeated until the cofferdam was full. A good weather window was necessary to plan this work.

Pier 17, the bridge's first foundation to be built, had a rather mysterious start when a crane operator, upon seeing the small narrow perch upon which he would work high above the water, quit his first day on the job. The crane later toppled over in a fierce windstorm. After the forms were in place and the stone was placed into a firm bed on the lake bottom, a marine grout plant was brought alongside to make grout from cement, sand, fly ash, and water. The mixture was then pumped through grout pipes that had been installed within, displacing the water and mixing with the stone to form a massive 170,000 ton block of solid concrete.

Preparations are being made to mount the huge steel eyebars deep in the anchor pier that will permanently hold the cables that will support the bridge. A phenomenal amount of pressure would soon be placed upon this anchor section, and it was necessary to check each step of the construction to insure that the integrity of the mass was intact. Core samples were drilled from the concrete after it was poured to be sure of the consistency. Later more stone was added to the base of the foundation and additional work done to the sheet piling. Steel braces were installed underwater in later years after the bridge opened to ensure that the pier stayed strong. Engineers detected minute movement within the foundation at one point, prompting the added work.

An identical pier was built on the north end of the suspended span, pier 22, and every detail was also checked in the construction of this massive block. However, pier 22's construction went smoothly and without incident. Few of the concerns that engineers had at pier 17 materialized at pier 22, even though it was built using the same methods and materials. Even today, a trip across the bridge provides no noticeable differences at pier 22 while a sudden "lift" effect can occur during windy conditions at pier 17. Engineers shake their heads today when asked about the differences in the two identical constructions, but point to the added stabilization at pier 17 as providing added assurance of the bridge's safety.

Once the basic form was completed for the anchor piers, a backstay support was put in place to link the anchor block to a cable-bent pier. This aerial view of the pier shows its hollow interior, where cables would someday be anchored. An icy winter failed to nudge the foundation from its location.

The completed pier is shown, with box-beam supports attached to both ends and cables anchored within. Exterior finishing was undertaken to create a smooth concrete finish on the outside of the block. The finished support allowed weight to be placed on the suspension cables, holding up the roadway supported by the giant towers.

The eyebars, embedded inside the concrete of pier 17 and pier 22, receive cabling spun in a 24-hour operation that had to continue until completion once started. The photograph at right shows the spinning wheel—which really only extended the cable and did not spin it at all—on one end of a run between the north and south anchor piers. Below is a view showing stands of cable packed together, creating the strength that would support the bridge road deck. It is here that the cables were looped onto the eyebar's ends, tying together the support system of the Mackinac Bridge.

Interior and exterior views of pier 17 reveal the suspension cable's theory of support. The interior view surprises many people, who do not realize that the huge concrete blocks are hollow. The cables are splayed out and attached to the eyebars, embedded in concrete. The exterior photograph shows the backstay span in place, with another frame being set in place to link to pier 16, not visible to the right. Note the presence of the cable-bent pier, known as pier 18. The bridge towers are up in this photograph, with the cables strung across their tops and readied for the job of supporting the roadway sections.

Four

TOWERING ABOVE

The most striking aspect of the Mackinac Bridge is the sight of the twin towers soaring above the Straits of Mackinac, supporting the bands of steel cable that hold more than a mile and a half of roadway aloft. The ivory columns symbolize two peninsulas, now joined by a magnificent bridge that carries everyday commerce, day travelers, vacationers, and local traffic between Mackinaw City and St. Ignace. The sight of the towers, which can be seen for many miles away on highway approaches to the area, instills excitement as a destination and hope as a waypoint on any Michigan journey from either north or south. At 552 feet tall above the waterline, the towers are within 3 feet of the height of the Washington Monument. However, the visible height is belied by the fact that each tower sits in 210 feet of water, added to the already impressive height. Then there is the additional 200 feet of the tower's foundation caissons that were drilled down to bedrock. Nearly 1,000 feet of structure stands at both the north and south tower locations—piers 19 and 20—to form the backbone of Dr. David B. Steinman's "net to catch the stars."

The sections for the caissons of the two main tower piers were fabricated at the Gary, Indiana, plant of United States Steel. They were then shipped in pieces to Alpena, Michigan, for assembly. Since these were to be sunk more than 200 feet below the surface of the straits, pre-fabricated, double-walled steel caissons measuring 116 feet in diameter were necessary.

Welders sealed the assembled pieces of the caissons to make them watertight between the walls. The walls were then divided into eight watertight compartments, creating a buoyant cylinder that would float. The plan was to move the caissons to the straits by towing them up Lake Huron—a journey of nearly 90 miles.

It was no wonder that someone referred to the caissons as "Paul Bunyan's doughnuts." After the rings were built to a height of 44 feet, a channel was dug from the big lake to the caisson, allowing it to float. They were then towed through the open channel and out onto the lake for the journey north. Sometimes the weather did not cooperate and the trip got a little rough, but each set of caissons arrived without casualty. The process was repeated until enough ring sections were completed to build the north and south caissons to their full heights. The caissons were an unusual sight on the lake for passing ships and pleasure boaters.

At the straits, the caissons met humble beginnings in the form of surveying towers, exactly the same beginning that the anchor blocks had when they were begun. To sink the giant rings into position, the space between the two circular steel walls was filled with rock aggregates to make them sink. Another double-walled ring of steel was then added to the top and then another, until the bottom reached the overburden at the bottom of the lake. The sand, mud, and stone of the overburden was dug out with clamshell buckets and dumped outside the caisson. The sharp, angled cutting edge penetrated through the overburden, until it dug firmly into bedrock.

The caissons for piers 19 and 20 were guided into place with the help of huge double-walled circular steel cans, constructed onshore and towed from St. Ignace to the tower locations. Cranes lifted additional circles to be fastened to the frames, until they were ready to be loaded onto a barge for the trip to the straits. Construction of this sort took place at the shoreline work site at St. Ignace, where crews built various sections of the bridge. These projects were vital to the time and economic constraints of the job and were mostly unseen by observers on the Lower Peninsula side.

Transporting the forms to the tower locations was always a concern when it came to weather. Calm seas in the bay could misrepresent conditions on the open water, but once the crews started the trip, they were on their way and reluctant to turn back. Accurate forecasts helped to ensure safe working conditions while handling tons of steel perched on barges floating at the mercy of the winds. Storms could keep the workmen ashore for days, but when everything calmed down the crews would return to the site and start where they had left off. Sometimes when a severe storm was reportedly coming in the crews would evacuate the work site, but many times the men worked in rain, wind, and snow.

The forms held four corral units, built up to the proper height and lowered to the overburden. The corrals were made of 20-inch pipes held together with 6-inch pipe bracing. Concrete was then pumped into the pipes for added strength to help hold it in position while being lowered to the bottom. They were then driven to rock and anchored with spud piles to secure the framework. They held the caissons in position from four corner positions. Two smaller cable-bent piers were also built in 1954, one with the caisson method and the other using a pair of cofferdams. The methods that were used differed due to contrasting conditions in tower locations.

This method of construction proved the naysayers wrong who predicted that the huge tower foundations would never make it through the many layers of overburden to substantial bedrock. The claims of undersea caverns vanished as the steel cutting edge of the caisson walls knifed down under the tremendous weight of the added layers of steel, reaching bedrock and cutting into a virtually eternal stronghold. Engineers had found their secure footings upon which to build the magnificent Mackinac Bridge. It was upon these foundations that Dr. David B. Steinman knew he could base nearly 100 million gross tons of superstructure, roadway, and traffic load. The key to his design would ultimately be flexibility and lack of resistance to wind, waves, and ice, but it was the secure and unwavering stronghold of the rock-solid foundations that ensured completion of the Mackinac Bridge project.

A new record for underwater consolidation of concrete was set in the spring of 1955, when work resumed after a long winter of ice and snow. During the 31 days of May that year, 103,000 cubic yards of concrete were poured into foundations of the Mackinac Bridge. The corral units were no longer needed as the caissons stood solidly on their own. From within, the circular design of the main cylinder of the caisson would arise two smaller pedestals, 38 feet in diameter, that would form the bases of the bridge towers. The pair of smaller cylinders began eight feet below the surface of the water, once the caissons were driven to their final depth.

On top of the steel and solid concrete caissons, main tower pedestals rose 25 feet above the water, their tops studded with steel bolts. The rows of bolts were carefully aligned to receive the next stage of the construction process. Thick base plates were fitted over the projecting fingers of steel, forming a junction of the concrete substructure and the steel superstructure into a permanent union. In doing so, this marriage of concrete and steel set the stage for ironwork to begin on the bridge above the waterline. The tower bases were now solid and ready to receive 552 feet of tower sections.

Another construction process involving the Mackinac Bridge was underway at the same time, but far from the usual building sites at St. Ignace or Mackinaw City. This work was being done 500 miles away, at Ambridge, Pennsylvania. The two towers that would support cables and roadway were being built horizontally and placed on the ground for final examination by fabricators and inspectors. The pieces of the towers were laid out on the ground and drift-pinned together to make sure that all the parts connected properly. Note the figures of workmen walking on the surface of the towers to determine the scale of the towers' size.

An advantage of the horizontal assembly process was that inspectors could see problems and correct them without holding up other phases of the work process. Another factor was the close proximity to the Pennsylvania fabrication plant, where steel was ready to be formed into parts and pieces that would do the job, rather than having to order the parts with measurements being taken hundreds of miles away. Being land-based gave the crews the advantage of creating the spires without the severe winter weather of the straits affecting timetables and work schedules. In retrospect, this process was one of many that saw the bridge completed on time and on budget.

After American Bridge inspectors determined that the pieces of the towers all were perfectly formed and fitted, the whole structure was disassembled and prepared for shipping. This lengthy process required the careful numbering and labeling of every part and piece to be assembled, no matter how small or how large. After the materials were all accounted for, it was another task altogether to get all the assembly pieces readied for transport by various shipping means. It took many loads of railroad cars, trucks and barges to move the tower sections from Pennsylvania to Michigan. Once they arrived, work crews began the process of taking inventory of all the parts and readying them for reassembly at St. Ignace. They did so knowing that the next assembly would be a vertical one and would be the one that would really count—for they would need to stand the test of elements and time.

On July 2, 1955, American Bridge began the gigantic task of erecting the steel superstructure of the world's longest suspension bridge. The first piece weighed 40 tons and represented the bottom 16 feet of a tower that would rise 552 feet above the water surface of the Straits of Mackinac.

When a floating derrick could no longer reach high enough to lift more pieces in place, a creeper derrick was built onto the tower itself to raise the next sections into place. Clinging to the side of the tower, it worked its way upward like an inchworm, gradually lifting steel sections weighing 80 tons more than one-tenth of a mile skyward.

As each piece was added to the tower, the general shape and look of the bridge began to take shape. Not much that had been done in the first year of construction had resembled anything similar to the bridge seen in the artists' concept drawings published in the newspapers. The towers, in particular, stood for progress among the public and the workers.

The struts that tied each tower section together were built of sturdy steel box sections, assuring absolute stability. Placing the heavy steel sections precisely in position required the best-skilled workmen and equipment available. It also took a lot of time. It was here, on the towers, that ironworkers began to really show their stuff.

In October 1955, the height of the towers reached 420 feet. The process involved the temporary bolting together of the sections until riveters caught up with the job of planting six million rivets designed to hold the towers together, driven from the outside but backed by workers stationed inside the columns.

As progress continued, workmen could see other pier sections underway as they came to work each day. By the end of the 1955 construction season, 27 additional foundations and their superstructures were built, ready for the assemblage of bridge sections—box beams that would support the roadway to be crossed by millions and millions of vehicles.

An impressive sight, the two Mackinac Bridge towers neared completion in the fall of 1955, almost ready for the next year's task of stretching cables across them. Many features had yet to be added, including elevators to transport workers aloft to do their jobs inside and outside the columns. For the time being, that trip was still being made via external hoisting apparatus that included wire cages to pull men up to their work stations. In addition, supplies and equipment had to be brought to the job site by boat and then distributed to the work crews by unconventional means. Safety was constantly emphasized, and the record shows that an amazing number of hours were worked safely in the most extreme of circumstances. Weather, water depth, and height were added factors of concern coupled with the heavy construction effort of building two complex towers that would be 552 feet tall.

The first of the towers were topped out on October 22, 1955. The height was comparable to that of the Washington Monument. An added feature came along later in the form of an 80-foot high guy derrick, ready for the next phase of construction. Workmen proudly displayed an American flag from the top of the structure they had worked so hard to build. The significance of that gesture was not lost on the engineering world, which at the time had again claimed the honor of building the longest suspension bridge in the world. It would take wider bodies of water to be crossed for anyone to beat what was being accomplished by the Mackinac Bridge, a feat that stood alone for 40 years.

The American ironworkers—men committed to doing a job right and not afraid of hard work. The crews that worked the inside of the towers, backing up rivets with hydraulic wrenches, were outfitted with the latest equipment of the times and bore helmet lights to see their way in the dark in much the same way that a miner would. It was the pure grit and determination that overcame harsh weather conditions, low morale due to accidents, and long shifts that kept them away from their families. Bone-tired and mentally weary, they still came back for more each day and were not satisfied until the job was done. Many of the men who worked on the Mackinac Bridge project in the 1950s have returned to the area over the years to admire their handiwork and show it off to friends and family—as they proudly should.

The effects of weather should not be underestimated in the toll it took on timing, work schedules, and especially the men who did the job. Storms buffeted the straits in the fall of 1955, with November gales producing high winds that tested the mettle of workers who needed to remember to tie things down. Waves smashed against the bridge tower foundations and coated them with ice, but did not in the least damage or nudge the structures. The construction plan was efficient, well founded, and well executed in that confidence grew as to the overall stability of the caissons and the other piers. Nature's ordinary behavior soon evolved into some of the most extreme conditions recorded to date in the winter of 1955, but the Mackinac Bridge remained resilient and unmoving in its resolve.

These two views of the north bridge tower display the status of the bridge's tower construction in 1956, mostly complete and becoming ready for sections to hang from the cables. Looking down from above, a barge is visible with construction supplies and materials available to workers. The suspender cables have been hung, and are awaiting a framework to be brought out from St. Ignace. The upward view shows the finished cables crossing the top of the tower, with a guy derrick still aloft. The contrasting views were likely seldom enjoyed by workmen, who often did not spend a lot of time looking up while working and knew better than to look down while working aloft.

There are seemingly an endless number of angles from which to photograph the Mackinac Bridge, and many scenes of the construction era examined the process from close up and far away. At close range, the still unpainted tower has been cleared of all derrick material atop the spire, and railing has been installed at each cross-section. From a distance, this shot of the bridge (undoubtedly taken earlier) reveals a string of cable across the straits with no sections of roadway support yet in place in the suspended stretch. Local boaters found a market in transporting photographers from various newspapers and magazines out to the bridge site for picture taking. Others did just fine from shore.

Another factor that figured in photographic success was the weather. A newspaper might send a staff photographer north to take pictures of the bridge on a day such as this, seen looking upward in the sunshine from the bridge deck. Under those conditions, possibilities were endless and editors were no doubt pleased by the return they reaped for the day's work. On other days, despite the sunshine on the mainland, there could be very foggy conditions at the straits in the vicinity of the bridge. This view from tower to tower shows a foggy situation that at least bares a landmark. On many days, especially in May and June, the fog is so thick that visibility could be cut to minimal extremes.

A trip to the top of the towers reveals a scene of solitude and wonder at the genius of Dr. David B. Steinman's design of the Mackinac Bridge, the respect for those who built it, and an appreciation for those who maintain it today. Even placid conditions below will often hide an appreciable increase in wind speed when aloft. Although the sounds of passing vehicles below can clearly be heard from the tops of the towers, the sounds of wind and the waves on the straits are just as noticeable. An inspiring view by any account, the trip to the top is well worth the climb in a phone-booth sized elevator that rises at approximately 100 feet per minute to the bottom of the top cross-section. A visitor must climb through a honeycombed network of steel girders before reaching a steel-runged ladder that is set in the tower wall. It is a vertical climb of 30 feet straight up before a submarine-type hatch opens to the top of the tower.

Five

A Suspended Span

The amount of steel cable used to support the suspended span of the Mackinac Bridge defies the imagination of any layman visualizing the materials needed to build a bridge of this size. Not only did spinning wheels extend four layers on each one-way trip across the suspension's length, but additional thicknesses of steel rope were braided to serve as suspender cables to actually hold up the box beams and the bridge deck. The cables have proven to possess more than adequate strength. A 1978 accident saw three U.S. Marine Corps reservists killed when their light plane became lost in the fog during a sightseeing detour and struck the suspender cables. The plane's wings were clipped off, but the cables only had scratches and paint marks on them. The flexible cables are routinely inspected for wear but continue to endure weather and load stress without appreciable maintenance concerns.

The 1955 bridge construction season saw buildings specially built in Sault Ste. Marie to store 55,500 coils of wire that had been shipped there for use in forming the cables of the Mackinac Bridge. Special machinery was brought in to splice the coils and wind them under precisely measured tension onto huge drums. Containing approximately 320,000 feet of wire, each reel weighed 16 tons. The wire measured .192 inches in diameter. Quite an operation took place at Sault Ste. Marie in preparing the wire for use. Quality control was a factor, and the timing of the wire production was a key in the success of the project.

Because the entire cable-spinning operation had to be done in one continuous process once it started, it was necessary for adequate supplies of the wire to be on hand for immediate use. The reels of wire were shipped to St. Ignace by rail and then returned empty immediately to prepare for the next trip. The simple diagram explaining cable spinning shows the route the wire took from a reel through a diesel engine drive that brought it through the eyebars embedded in concrete and on to an endless hauling rope for the journey over two towers and through the next anchor pier. The process was then shifted off the wheel and back in the other direction in reverse.

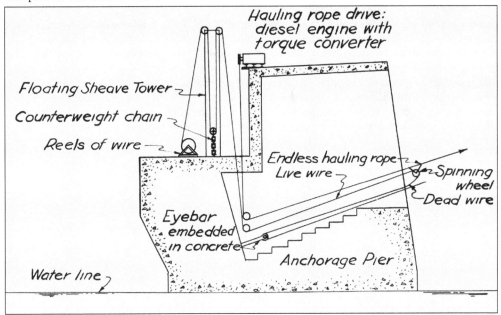

This dramatic view shows the perch workmen used at the beginning of the cable-spinning process. A platform was necessary for the men to use while binding and clamping the cables and later attaching the guides for the suspender cables. Chain-link fence was stretched along the five wire ropes strung as guidelines, stiffened by 8-by-10-inch wooden planks every few feet. The fencing, unfolded in bundles, became a catwalk that would support human weight and more. The trick was to gently slide the bundles out and down the slope, connected on all sides by the wire rope. Two men died on their first day on the job when a rope that restrained the bundles snapped, causing them to fall into the straits from a height of more than 500 feet in the air. In all, five lives were lost during the Mackinac Bridge construction project.

This is the view, "down the slope," as seen by workmen. Chain-link fence is being installed to form a catwalk to prepare for cable spinning. The job entailed stretching the fencing tight, securing the sides with clamps, and then building the cross-ties between the five wire ropes for support. It was a work-as-you-build-it process that required concentration, strength, and precision while working at very dangerous heights. A dropped tool, a slip of the foot, or a loose grip could have fatal consequences. The job was definitely not for the faint at heart. Wind and temperature variances increased the risk, as did rainfall and dew, which created extremely slick surfaces. Unlike federal requirements that demand safe practices today, workmen of that era prided themselves on working unsecured, without the benefit of a safety belt or clamped restraint. They complained that it took too long to tie them on and off. Some workmen said that taking the time to use such a device then would be a sure ticket to getting fired from the job.

As workmen unfolded the bundles of fencing much like a road map, they gradually got to the point where the angle was not so severe and the job became more routine. Consider that they looked at working more than 200 feet above an open air space—with water below that was 300 feet deep—as routine. As each bundle stretched farther and farther across the abyss, the progress brought more and more workmen aloft to take on other aspects of the job to prepare for the cables. Soon a crew from the other side was visibly approaching towards the center of the span.

When at last bridge workers met in the middle, the catwalk had been completed connecting anchorage to anchorage and readying the route for the cable spinning. Some of the as yet unsecured fencing created a bouncy effect when the workmen walked from section to section, but they took it in stride and seemed as at ease as anyone doing their job at street level. By now, the crews were also installing side posts to hold additional cabling as rails for further protection. The dizzying heights still seem incredible, even when viewed as photographs; today there are 1,300 drivers per year who request help driving them across the bridge. The Mackinac Bridge offers a motorist-assist program that provides a driver for cars, motorcycles, and even tractor-trailer drivers who cannot cope with the thought of driving across the bridge.

Bridge workers were used to dealing with the exorbitant heights of their job on a daily basis. Perhaps there was safety in numbers, but mostly they seemed too intent on getting their jobs done to worry about where they were working. The more work they did the catwalk, the safer and sturdier it became. Sometimes the way to do the job was to lay down, and other times, the workmen sat or kneeled to attain maximum angles for torque or comfort. In addition to the standard safety helmet, work boots and a good set of gloves were needed on the job. Wood cleats were wired to the fence floor to secure a safer walking surface. Steel trusses were used to connect the catwalks for additional steadiness. The catwalks were primarily completed one side at a time, but finished with all the extra features together to be ready for the cable-spinning operation.

The actual cable spinning operation entailed two wheels that extended—and did not really spin, braid, or twist—the cable from one anchorage to another. Each trip took about 12 minutes and added four cables to the band per wheel, constantly increasing its strength. The wheels ran in opposite directions and pulled the same amount of cable on each run, thanks to a tensioning device.

When the two wheels met in the middle, it proved the preciseness of the operation. Cowbells were installed in the wheels to warn workmen of the approaching equipment, which could knock a man off his feet if he did not see it coming. A friendly rivalry developed between 300 men working two shifts to see which crew could string the most cable.

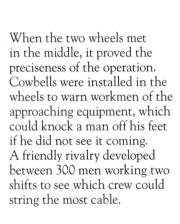

Each trip by the double-grooved spinning wheel laid down four wires to be included in a strand of 340 wires. The 24.25-inch main suspension cable was made up of 37 strands. When the wheel reached the anchor pier, the wires were transferred to strand shoes and another set looped around for the trip in the opposite direction.

The cable spinning also took place at night. The crews worked in two 10-hour shifts and succeeded in spinning 41,000 miles of cable wire without a hitch. Another 1,000 miles were used to create the suspender cables then dropped from the main cables to support the roadway sections.

Cross trusses were attached to both catwalks, further stiffening the walkways and allowing quick access to the other side. Storm guys were also installed to keep the catwalk connections from swaying in high winds. This allowed men to keep working even though the winds may have come up.

The ever-increasing number of wires near the walkways caused bridge workmen to carefully consider their route of travel while walking about. Staying in the cable lane was important to avoid tripping over a set and suffering the consequences. No one was seriously hurt in this manner.

Bridge workers carefully adjusted every wire that was pulled across the suspension span by the wheel. They usually did this procedure at night when the wires were less likely to contract or expand due to the position of the sun and varying temperatures. The process was completed five strands of wire at a time. A variety of tools and equipment were used during this phase of the operation, but most workers relied upon human strength, patience, and concentration to keep the wires consistent in their placing and grouping into strands. A mix-up meant getting reorganized and starting over before the next wheel arrived with more wire.

Once the cable wires were grouped into strands, the crew then had to group the strands together for eventual formation into the 37 strands that would make up the full cable, which measured 24.25 inches in diameter. The cables were separated into strand groups that could be more easily worked with, but that process had to be completed all the way up and down the length of the cable route. It was a time-consuming process that required exacting attention to detail. Soon the entire length of the cable route was ready for banding and compressing together into one strong team of cables.

The timing of the cable spinning operation allowed for multitasking the process as it was taking place on the catwalks. Workmen adjusted, compressed, and banded the strands on one cable while the spinning process was taking place on the other. The teamwork involved in the transfer of duties kept everyone on their toes. In addition, the frequent change of jobs helped to keep the workers mentally alert during the shift, a factor unseen on a more redundant, laborious task. All in all, the way the men did their jobs made the cable spinning operation much safer than it could have ordinarily been.

The next step was to prepare the completed full cables for banding and hydraulic compression. The past 78 days had proven effective in stringing the wire, but now it needed to be prepared to handle the load of the bridge's weight. Temporary bands were installed to group the large cable sections together in one smooth line. The individual attention paid to each wire along the way allowed for the same amount of tension and load distribution among them all. Careful measurements were taken to ensure that this was so. All the work was done at the same incredible heights, and some involved moving heavy machinery out onto the catwalks for duty.

The permanent bands were then installed, using hydraulic equipment that was cumbersome to move about but necessary to do the job. As winter approached, work crews competed with falling temperatures to tighten the cable strands into one perfectly rounded shape that would eventually support the suspender cables. The compression and banding process had to be accomplished along the entire length of the suspension cables' route, and each circle of thin wire had to be applied precisely to guarantee total uniformity of its load-bearing capacity. As the process was nearing completion, the bridge workers could at last see a restful winter ahead following their successful season of work.

Mackinac Bridge workers, like many workers involved in an intense high-stakes project, enjoyed a special camaraderie that they still speak of today. There was a feeling of togetherness, of them all being in the same situation, and of beating the odds. There was also a concern for each others' safety and welfare, with many of the men becoming life-long friends. This is evident in the attendance at the annual Ironworkers Festival, held each August in Mackinaw City, where members of various union locals gather from around the country to partake in skill contests and recall old times. As the years have gone by, fewer and fewer of the attendees have been men who worked on the building of the Mackinac Bridge. The ones who now attend after more than a half-century since their days on the Straits are treated as celebrities by the much younger workers from other projects across America.

After the cables were permanently wrapped in protective wire, the suspender cables were attached to hold up the bridge roadway. These cables were made from the five wire ropes that had initially supported the catwalks. They had been removed, stretched and cut to specific lengths, and capped. These cables form the "harp strings" of the bridge's suspension system. Each had to be looped over the main cable and placed into a guiding fitting grooved across the top of the main cables. They then hung downward to await the arrival of the bridge sections the following spring. Work was done to admit the suspender cables through the catwalks that had been stretched and secured into place for safety.

The location of the bridge worker, high above the straits, could be a lonely place at times when a man was left to do a specific job alone. But the jobs were all part of a tremendous effort to suspend a roadway high above a deep channel nearly five miles across. The diagram shows the details involved in the supporting process of holding up that roadway. Lifting struts would help erect stiffening trusses from a material barge that had floated it out from the shore. Two four-drum hoisting engines powered the work. The design included some 3,800 feet of the bridge's suspended span.

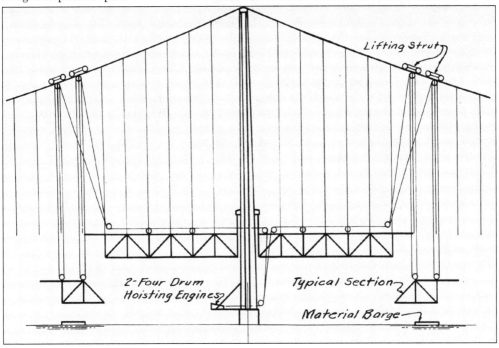

Lifting Strut

2-Four Drum Hoisting Engines

Typical Section

Material Barge

As workmen raced to finish the cable and suspender cable projects, the onset of winter made for some uncomfortable working conditions high above the straits. This photograph shows a crew aloft in cold winds and snowy conditions, a weather pattern not at all unusual for late November or early December at Mackinac. The idea that these men are using a hydraulic jack to tighten the fittings for the suspender cables at clearly more than 400 feet above the water lends perspective to the resolve these workmen had. Note the layered clothing and gloves and the precarious footing involved in the job on such a cold day. Yet they had to handle heavy tools, install parts, and be able to apply force and nimble adjustments all in the same frozen shift. Remarkably, none of the major accidents that occurred during construction took place during the change of seasons to winter weather.

A final step before the cables were encased in a protective piping was to coat the wires in a corrosive-resistant, "red-lead" paste. This was done to protect against rust and corrosion, two factors which could seriously compromise the integrity of the suspension system. The coating was a terrific success, as annual inspections done by removing the piping reveal little to no damage done by the forces of nature. The cables were banded together properly in the first place and then treated in such a way as to offer long-term protection. After more than a half-century of use, the fact that they are in such great shape bodes well for the ultimate lifespan of the bridge. The cables are one of the only parts of the bridge not on a designated replacement program list. They need to stay in tip-top condition.

Today the Mackinac Bridge cables are walked by maintenance workers who change the light bulbs, replace the colored globes, and check for signs of stress and wear. It is still an unusual job but one that today is always done with a safety harness that clips the worker to the lead cable. Although the angle gets appreciably steeper as the approach to each tower is made, the maintenance workers today use this method of travel to access their locations. When replacing bulbs or globes, workmen are seen using a newspaper carrier's delivery bag, provided by the Sault Evening News of Sault Ste. Marie. The canvas bag is perfect for storing the glass items while aloft and provides easy access to replacements.

Six

BUILT ASHORE, JOINED IN THE STRAITS

Besides the main suspension span, the Mackinac Bridge is really constructed of a series of smaller, conventional bridges that would span many wide, formidable rivers and gorges. The building of these linked spans took place for the most part on land. The giant box beam sections were then towed out from shore on barges and lifted into place by cranes. Crews of ironworkers riveted the pieces together to form the complete link between the Upper and Lower Peninsulas of Michigan. Only then could road crews come in to lay forms for pouring concrete and layering asphalt for traffic to drive on. The parade of tugboats that delivered each carefully measured section to its place in the puzzle was quite a sight for "shoreline superintendents" who marveled at the techniques and methods used in building the bridge. All the work was done within sight of ferryboat passengers, crossing for the last 35-minute trips before they would be able to drive across the new route in less than 10 minutes. Michigan's miracle bridge was becoming a reality.

Plenty of steel frame construction continued to take place at St. Ignace, where barges, tugboats, cranes, and other heavy equipment worked to build the bridge sections that would later be towed out into the straits for placement and assembly. The two-lane roadways leading to Moran Bay became busy thoroughfares used by workmen driving to the job and equipment operators attending to their job sites. The frozen bay slept for the winter, but on-shore construction continued as seen in this photograph. Note the ice fishing shanties at right. Locals were not disrupted in some of their favorite pastimes, and fished next to bridge sections weighing thousands of tons. Bridge watching was an activity that could be viewed from the shore, but in St. Ignace there was plenty to see in the water right off State Street. The partially completed bridge can be seen above, off the shoreline towards Mackinaw City.

The gritty determination of the ironworker is seen in the faces of these men heading to work aboard a tugboat at dawn. Workers were issued a safety helmet complete with miner's light and a life jacket for the boat trip out to the job site. Beyond that, all they took along was their lunch. Incredibly the men left the life jackets onboard the boat for the next crew, disregarding the fact that they were all working around very deep water that could be extremely cold. A missed step could become a fatal mistake, but little protection was offered or accepted. During construction, a laborer from St. Ignace lost his life when he fell off a girder just four feet above the water and drowned. Travel across the water by boat each day was part of the job and part of life on the Mackinac Bridge project.

An aerial view taken during construction of the Mackinac Bridge shows a line of stepping stones across the Straits of Mackinac. All 34 of the bridge's pier foundations were in place at this point, with workmen getting down to business on the smaller support piers that would comprise foundations for individual bridge sections.

A close-up photograph of one of the smaller piers for the bridge is seen here, founded on bedrock and built with two columns from just below the waterline. The forms were gradually built up to the height needed, and every one of them was part of a natural progression of the bridge's inclination angle.

As bridge foundations rose to greater heights, they were prepared to receive the steel forms that would eventually support the roadway. Concrete workers were at their best during this phase of the bridge's construction, paying meticulous attention to detail and making sure that each column's diameter was exactly as specified.

The biggest things to ever be built or seen in St. Ignace were the stiffening trusses and backstay spans that would support the road deck between the cable-bent piers and the anchor blocks. Weighing 720 tons, the trusses measured 472 feet long and were mounted on falsework that stood 80 feet high above the ground.

Each backstay span was mounted on two barges that were tied together for the job of transporting them to the job site. The top-heavy forms were carefully balanced, but many feared that they would blow over at the dock in St. Ignace, before ever having a chance to be riveted to the bridge. On November 16, 1955, a blizzard with winds as strong as 76 miles per hour nearly took over, but the shelter of the bay saved it. Only three days later, everything had calmed down, and the enormous framework was towed across calm seas to its permanent home attached to pier 17, the bridge's south anchor pier.

The operation of moving a backstay span to the straits for duty at the anchor pier had the full attention of the Merritt-Chapman and Scott crews the day the work was done. Several tugboats were employed to push where needed and slowly inch the form—larger than many highway bridges across major rivers—into position. As workmen waited, winches were used to pull from many directions to ensure stability. Such a large piece could suffer a disastrous end if it were to topple, endangering many lives. Finally everything lined up, and the backstay was a perfect fit into a steel shoe. The truss was secured with a 500-pound pin hammered into place until the rest of the connections could be made. The falsework below still had to be removed, so once all was tight up above, water was flooded into the two transport barges until the falsework could be towed out from under the new bridge section.

Other construction work was underway on land, in addition the pieces to be towed out to the straits. The general highway approach to the bridge was being formed at Mackinaw City, where a viaduct took the highway over the village's main street, Central Avenue. Homes were moved or torn down to make way for the new bridge. Several streets were cut off and renamed with "east" or "west" designations. Approach ramps were also being built at St. Ignace, where road graders carved a highway out of a steep hill overlooking the straits. An interchange with two exit ramps and an entrance ramp would later be built from this area.

One type of support used for the smaller bridge supports were H sections, positioned along the shallower shoreline areas where the bridge's inclination was not yet very high compared to the rest of the span. Many workmen are seen atop this section, preparing it to accept a steel bridge frame.

The other type of support used for elevating roadways at Mackinac Bridge was a T section, sometimes called "elephant ears" by the bridge crews. They were taller than the H sections, usually were founded in deeper water, and held the bridge at a higher inclination. Each type of support had to hold up thousands of tons of steel, concrete, and bridge traffic.

The partially completed approach section from the Mackinaw City shore is seen in this aerial photograph, clearly showing the angle of inclination the new span would assume. The sharp angle was only the beginning, for the suspended portion was a much steeper ride uphill. Note the fort along the shoreline, just above the bridge.

This view looking north towards St. Ignace displays a nicely lined row of T sections, supporting the bridge framework before pier 22, the north anchor block. The Mackinac Bridge offers many examples of symmetry and geometric angles, and photographs of the bridge could be used to teach many mathematics classes at various levels of study.

The process of "cooking" rivets was performed by ironworkers throughout the process of building the Mackinac Bridge. A small but intense heat stove took the iron rivet and heated it until white hot, perfect for bonding into metal prepared to be linked. Ironworkers would toss the rivets to partners nearby who would catch them in a wide leather cone shaped like a megaphone, easily deposited into the waiting hole for bonding. A pressurized hydraulic tube could also be used to transport the "hot potatoes" on longer journeys. Masters of their craft, ironworkers display these skills today in competitions at Mackinaw City's Ironworkers Festival each August.

Stiffening truss sections were moved to the straits and mounted on H sections and T sections as the bridge grew longer from each shoreline. Some observers thought that traffic would be inside a formation such as this one, not realizing that the roadbed would be supported above these cavernous frames.

Another challenge faced by engineers was having to raise each stiffening truss only when it was needed to offset the weight of another, avoiding an imbalance that would have caused big trouble. The forms still looked out of balance at times, since the contour of the bridge did not take its final shape until the full load had been applied.

Radio communication played an important role in the positioning of the stiffening trusses, as did old-fashioned hand signals. Crane operators, ironworkers, tugboat captains, foremen, and winch-haulers all had to communicate to ensure safety and smooth operations. The high-stakes balancing act that was played out on the straits provided many, many hours of entertainment for observers on the shore. Some days, people claimed there was nobody working on the bridge when in reality hundreds were. Other days, the dramatic show went on from dawn until dusk. Pay-to-use telescopes mounted in parks onshore did a brisk business as the bridge neared completion.

Finally the day came when there was only one small section needed to connect the Mackinac Bridge framework, thus completing the suspension span that had for so long been dreamed of and talked about by state leaders and businessmen. The timing of this event placed it at the height of the tourist season in late July during 1957, the final year of construction. Two stiffening trusses had been raised at each cable-bent pier and another at the center of the bridge. Although the bridge's roadway was far from completion, the significance of finishing the box beam sections of the bridge's framework drew plenty of attention, as it was apparent that the link between the Upper and Lower Peninsulas would soon be passable by automobile. The opening of the bridge was still scheduled for November 1, but workmen faced a nearly impossible schedule to finish on time.

The date was July 22, 1957, and inclement weather delayed the raising of the final piece of Dr. David B. Steinman's geometric puzzle to conquer the Straits of Mackinac. Winds were the chief issue, causing wave action that endangered the success of raising the final center section. Among the expectant crowds who watched were 75 news correspondents who waited, and waited, and waited. As the day went on, bridge construction officials were determined that improving conditions would allow them to get the job done. Finally that evening, the last section was raised and bolted into place, connecting the steel of a bridge that would tie Michigan together as a state.

Mackinac Bridge crews wasted no time in utilizing the newly completed link. Decking was immediately installed on each side of the towers for 80 feet, providing a work platform that served as the start of carpentry operations to build forms for the laying of concrete. Roadway stringers were brought out to be bolted into place. The steel frames of the bridge would now be covered by decking along its five-mile length. The sounds of riveters and crane operators were soon replaced by the pounding of nails and sawing of boards to use in the forms. It was a different type of work than had been prevalent for the previous three years, but its necessity meant that the bridge was close to being finished. It was time to put in a roadway.

The ironworkers stayed just ahead of the carpenters in bringing in the roadway stringers and tightening them into place to support the roadway decking. Hydraulic equipment was used for some aspects of the job, but old-fashioned elbow grease was best for other situations. The carpenters placed forms for the concrete roadbed, knowing that there were other workmen right behind them ready to pour cement and complete the next phase of the project. The teamwork among all work crews was vital to finishing the project on time, with an opening date just three months away. November 1 loomed just ahead with so much yet to be done.

Cement workers lay re-rod and pour forms that will become the roadway of the Mackinac Bridge. Much of the cement work was generated at Mackinaw City by the Catsman Company, which built a plant there specifically for the bridge job. Many varieties of jobs came to the area for subcontractors in these areas. Just ahead of the cement workers and carpenters, ironworkers continually placed roadway stringers for the next mile of the bridge until it was all finished. Many large pieces of heavy equipment could now be used on the bridge deck and work progressed rapidly in the race against time.

All suspension bridges are designed to move to accommodate wind, temperature change, and weight. Thanks to the open grating installed on the middle two lanes of the Mackinac Bridge, the design flexes easily when necessary. There are two large finger joints at the towers to accommodate all the expansion of the suspended spans. There are 11 smaller finger joints and 5 sliding joints across the bridge. In addition, there are 13 expansion joints for the south viaduct spans, 1 for each of these simple spans. This adds up to a total of 31 total joints. Wind water and snow easily passes through the grated surface.

Due to the flexible design of the bridge's construction, it is possible that the deck at center span could move as much as 35 feet (east or west) due to high winds. This would only happen under severe wind conditions. The deck would not swing or "sway" but rather move slowly in one direction based on the force and direction of the wind. After the wind subsides, the weight of the vehicles crossing would slowly move it back into center position. This could take days. The movements also are affected by temperature, with each difference of a few degrees raising or lowering the suspended cables in minute amounts.

Foundations and footings are underway in this photograph of the beginnings of the Mackinac Bridge Authority Administration Building. The same type of limestone that was used in the construction of the bridge was used to build this building. Still to come were maintenance facilities and the tollbooths. The Mackinac Bridge Authority's offices included a basement and underground vault, a conference room, operations center, and multiple work spaces for staff members. Note the presence of the surveyor's tower near the middle of the entrance ramp, kept in place until all factions of the bridge lined up through three seasons of construction in all sorts of weather. Plenty of concrete work was yet to be done at the time of this photograph, with 10 lanes of highway to be completed across the tollbooth entrances. The extra space allowed for vehicles to enter the administration building area and a breakdown lane.

The completed tollbooth and administration building were readied just in time for occupancy before the Mackinac Bridge opened for business. The wood-paneled conference room featured a fireplace and an awesome view of the bridge from a set of southern windows. The tollbooths were designed to serve traffic out either side, depending on which direction traffic flowed. A lighted sign was activated by the cash registers, allowing an operations supervisor inside the administration building to see what the collector had charged the vehicle's driver. This process is logged today into a computer for immediate reference. Intercoms have also been installed for immediate communication between operations personnel and fare collectors.

The last job to get the Mackinac Bridge ready for traffic was to coat the concrete traffic lanes with a layer of bituminous asphalt, completed only days before the official opening. Bridge workers were commended for their resolve in completing each job under tremendous pressure to have everything ready for the first day of business. Another winter was coming up, and jobs such as asphalting did not have much leeway before temperatures would be too cold to be effective. The entire state and much of the world had heard about the new bridge, and officials wanted to be sure there were no last minute snags to prevent a smooth first impression for travelers and visitors to the ceremonies.

Overhead highway lighting was installed to make nighttime crossings of the bridge safe and enjoyable. The bridge lighting could be seen for miles from either the Mackinaw City or St. Ignace shores, and cable lighting provided a further distinctive accent. A daytime view of the bridge was dramatic enough, but the images seen after dark sparked a rush in evening photography in the area for postcards, magazine covers, and portraits of the bridge. Both amateur and professional cameramen pursued many angles, and all found that there were many facets to viewing the bridge—none of them a bad shot.

One thing that bridge workers did not do before the bridge opened was paint it. The construction schedule dictated a November opening, and painters needed warmer temperatures before they could begin the big job of painting such a large structure. In addition, weather extremes at that time of year and beyond into winter made it far too dangerous to have painters aloft or working on the span when the job could wait until the following summer. The plan became to have the paintwork done the next year. During the first winter of operation, the Mackinac Bridge stood proudly in its newborn color of "red-lead," a coating applied by ironworkers during fabrication to protect it from corrosion and rust. The color is different from the "international orange" of the Golden Gate Bridge in San Francisco Bay. The color seen during the first winter at Mackinac Bridge was only a primer of sorts.

The bridge underwent painting in its forest green and ivory colors in the spring of 1958. It was a smooth process of simply applying paint over primer. Every summer since, some portion of the bridge has undergone a sanding and painting process that has been a never-ending job for more than 50 years. Weather permitting, the Mackinac Bridge is paintable if it is warmer than 40 degrees with low humidity and wind velocities are within safety margins to have workmen on the bridge. In the 1980s, for example, it was estimated that it took 40,000 gallons of paint and eight summers to finish the bridge from one end to the other. Then they would start over again. Today the process takes about a year less.

Seven

TWO PENINSULAS JOINED

On November 1, 1957, traffic officially opened on the Mackinac Bridge. A huge story, the event attracted 150 newspapermen from throughout Michigan and neighboring states that included Wisconsin, Illinois, Ohio, Indiana, New York, and Ontario. The Associated Press and United Press International opened offices in the area, and *Life Magazine*, the *New York Times*, and *Chicago Tribune* sent reporters. Detroit radio station WJR sent a mobile broadcasting unit in a specially equipped bus to beam the proceedings back to Detroit for broadcast throughout the Midwest. Invitations were accepted by 50 members of the Michigan Legislature, the *Cheboygan Daily Tribune* reported. Speeches were made on pier 22, the bridge's north anchor block, declaring the straits to be conquered at last for automobile traffic. With the ferries stopped and the bridge barricaded, cars were lined up at the bridge from the north and the south. Traffic was waiting at the St. Ignace end for a mile and a half, and at the Mackinaw City approach for two miles. The first official bridge fare was paid by Gov. G. Mennen Williams, who was driven across by his wife, Nancy. At St. Ignace, scores of legislators, newspapermen, and official guests waited for the official opening.

A Michigan State Police officer waiting at Mackinaw City received the notice to remove barriers from the traffic lanes, and cars began streaming across. That was the culmination of 70 years of talking and dreaming about a straits bridge, of discouraging attempts in the legislature and in Congress to get the bridge approved, of efforts to raise the funds, and finally of a three-year construction program necessary for the world's longest and costliest (to date) bridge. Michigan was indeed one.

The first official bridge fare was paid by Michigan governor G. Mennen Williams, who was driven across by his wife, Nancy. At St. Ignace, scores of legislators, newspapermen and official guests waited for the official opening. At 2:00 p.m., Governor Williams arrived from Mackinaw City in a limousine in front of the toll plaza at the north end of the bridge. Waiting for him was chairman Prentiss M. Brown of the Mackinac Bridge Authority, with a borrowed toll collector's cap on his head. The chairman held out his hand, and the governor handed him an oversized check made out for $3.25. Ceremonial protocol aside, everyone crossing the bridge had to pay, and there have never been arrangements made to accept a check at the tollbooths. But this was left for the accountants to decide, as Brown then nodded to a state trooper, who relayed the word through the radio in his car to open the bridge.

When the bridge was opened to traffic, the straits ferry fleet stopped forever. One era opened in history as another ended. When the barriers were removed, there was a traffic jam on the bridge as cars arrived faster than toll collectors could take their money. With the bridge open, a less joyous program began of bidding goodbye to the ferry crewman, some of whom started work the next day for the Mackinac Bridge Authority in various jobs. The *Vacationland* was the last ferry to cross, arriving in Mackinaw City with a full load of invited guests and newsmen covering the angle of the ferry system ending service. Some motorists continued to arrive at the dock to cross the straits, but were told to go to the bridge. The ferries were tied up for good, and the Mackinac Bridge was now open for business.

The first public fare to be accepted at the tollbooths after Gov. G. Mennen Williams was from Al Carter, a jazz band drummer from Chicago who made a hobby of being first at various events. Carter had been in line since the night before the bridge opened in order to be the first to cross. For a time, Carter's car was displayed at the bridge on the St. Ignace side, and at one point, Carter wanted to give the car a glorious send-off by having it dropped from the middle of the bridge into the straits. This plan met with general approval as a publicity stunt but eventually raised the ire of environmentalists who successfully blocked the idea on the grounds that it would pollute the waters during an era when many states were working to clean up the Great Lakes. The car Carter used is now displayed in the Grand Rapids Historical Museum.

Only a comparative few of the thousands of people attending the celebration were able to watch the dedication of the Mackinac Bridge, held at pier 22, the north anchor block of the bridge, on June 28, 1958. It was there that a five-mile length of ribbon was stretched from Mackinaw City at the south end and from the St. Ignace shore to the north. The four-inch ribbon was unwound from large spools and attached to the side-view mirrors of the convertibles of 83 Michigan county queens until the ends met, a process that took 25 minutes. There the ribbons were tied by the wives of Governor Williams and chairman Prentiss M. Brown, symbolizing that Michigan's two peninsulas were tied together as one by the bridge. Access to the Saturday bridge dedication ceremonies was by invitation only. Members of the public were able to hear the proceedings through a public address system set up at exhibit areas in both St. Ignace and Mackinaw City.

A magnificent fireworks display was set off on both Thursday and Friday nights at both Mackinaw City and St. Ignace. Each city had its display at the Mackinac Bridge shoreline. The St. Ignace display was first each night at 9:30 p.m., with Mackinaw City's starting at 10:00 p.m. In all, 600 varieties of fireworks were used and touched off 12 American flags. Military displays and other exhibits were located on the state ferry docks at Mackinaw City and St. Ignace. Approximately 2,500 men of the armed forces took part in the event. Two hundred National Guardsmen pitched camp at Mackinaw City High School. A destroyer escort and five patrol craft assembled and were joined by three Coast Guard cutters. Helicopter crews demonstrated air-sea rescues. Civil Air Patrol planes landed on the ferry dock at Mackinaw City in a demonstration of pinpoint landing techniques. At night, the ships played their searchlights on the Mackinac Bridge.

Parades that were held during the Mackinac Bridge Dedication Festival were the longest and most beautiful ever held to date in the area. With 140 units accepted for review, the parades marched through St. Ignace and Mackinaw City, with a glorious trip across the bridge. The parades were led by color guards of the U.S. Army, U.S. Air Force, U.S. Marines, U.S. Navy, Coast Guard, and Civil Air Patrol. Approximately 20 bands played, including the 5th Army Band. Numerous queens took part, representing all 83 Michigan counties and numerous festivals throughout the state. Among them were Miss Mackinaw City, Miss St. Ignace, Miss Michigan, Mrs. Michigan, and Miss Armed Forces. Also present were the Michigan Apple Queen, the Michigan Bean Queen, the Michigan Cherry Queen, and the Michigan Dairy Princess. The Oldsmobile Company and the Ford Motor Company donated white convertibles for use. Oxen teams, antique automobiles, motorcycle units, and Detroit mounted policemen represented other varieties of transportation.

Many beautiful floats were involved in the Mackinac Bridge Dedication Festival parades, including local entries from nearly all area communities in the northern part of the state. This entry was from the twin communities of Sault Ste. Marie, Michigan, and Sault Ste. Marie, Ontario, Canada. Neighboring communities were eager to show their support and appreciation for the new Mackinac Bridge. Each Michigan county in the Upper Peninsula supplied a representative car to cross, declaring its name and claim to fame on a sign. The access to the Upper Peninsula via the bridge was seen as an economic boon to the communities there. Mrs. Michigan Barbara Dolan rode through the streets and across the bridge in the festivities.

Local queens honored in the Mackinac Bridge Dedication Festival parades included Miss Mackinaw City Diane Krueger, and Miss St. Ignace Lenore Allen. People lined the streets of the two communities and waited at the entrances of the bridge to see the cars come across. Various commemorative events also took place during the celebration. On Friday, the trip of Jean Nicolet, the first European to visit the straits, was reenacted. Two champion canoeists set out from the beach at Mackinaw City at 10:00 a.m. in a birch-bark canoe, while another laden with beaver skins was paddled from the Upper Peninsula shore by two Native American canoeists. The two canoes met under the center of the bridge. A marker was unveiled at the Michilimackinac State Park to commemorate the establishment of a fort at Mackinaw City by the French in 1712.

The opening of the new bridge symbolized a new era for tourism and invited vacationers to come north to partake in the many recreational activities offered. Michigan's Upper Peninsula was already well known for its summertime boating, camping, and beaches. The state wanted to emphasize the availability of winter sports too and promoted snowmobiling and skiing using the bridge as part of the invitation. The attraction developed into a whole new industry for Upper Peninsula businesses and those in the northern Lower Peninsula. Today the bridge continues as a transportation link for those who journey north for winter recreational pursuits.

There are many jobs to be done to keep the Mackinac Bridge operating smoothly. As long as it costs money to cross it, there will always be a need for toll collectors to accept cash, tokens, and fare cards and perform any number of extra tasks that must be performed on a daily basis. Collecting money is the obvious job of the toll collector, and at first glance most people probably think that it would be the most boring job in the world. At times, it can be. But anyone who has stayed with the job for more than one summer's worth of employment will tell you that "minding the Mac" has its moments of excitement, comedy, frustration, and gratification. The people who have served in this position over the years are a loyal, cohesive crew that takes care of "their" bridge. In the early days, the uniform included a coat, tie, and collector's cap.

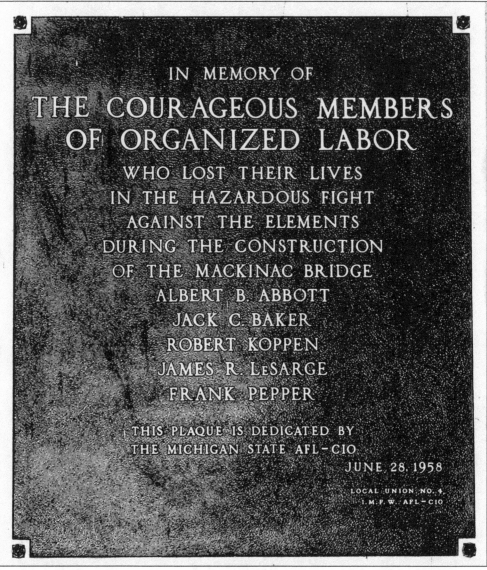

IN MEMORY OF
THE COURAGEOUS MEMBERS
OF ORGANIZED LABOR
WHO LOST THEIR LIVES
IN THE HAZARDOUS FIGHT
AGAINST THE ELEMENTS
DURING THE CONSTRUCTION
OF THE MACKINAC BRIDGE
ALBERT B. ABBOTT
JACK C. BAKER
ROBERT KOPPEN
JAMES R. LeSARGE
FRANK PEPPER

THIS PLAQUE IS DEDICATED BY
THE MICHIGAN STATE AFL-CIO
JUNE 28, 1958

LOCAL UNION NO. 4
I. M. F. W. AFL-CIO

A rule of thumb in heavy construction work estimates that one life will be lost for every $10 million spent. Predictions of up to 10 fatalities likely to occur during the building of the bridge were swelled by the extreme depths and exorbitant heights to assume that a dozen men would be lost during the three years it would take to build the five-mile span. In fact, the lives of five workmen were lost during the construction of the bridge between 1954 and 1957. Another, Daniel Doyle, died during maintenance work in 1997. Each a heartbreaking tragedy, the number was far below what was predicted by the rule of thumb forecast by those in the industry, making the building and day-to-day work performed on the Mackinac Bridge quite safe in retrospect. A plaque was dedicated in 1958 at the base of the bridge in Mackinaw City to honor those who had made the supreme sacrifice. A street in front of the bridge's maintenance facility was named for Doyle.

Eight

BRIDGING MICHIGAN'S FUTURE

Truly the Straits of Mackinac epitomizes the state motto of Michigan, *Si quaeris peninsulam amoenam, circumspice*, or "If you seek a pleasant peninsula, look about you." The Mackinac Bridge celebrated 50 years of service in 2007 after first opening to traffic on November 1, 1957. Indeed Michigan's greatest symbol deserved plenty of fanfare and honors. The bridge that Dr. David B. Steinman designed to last more than 1,000 years had weathered its first 50 years in glorious fashion. Expertly maintained, fully funded, and amazingly resilient to the many forces and factors of man and nature that had failed to seriously affect its status as the lone highway link between Michigan's two main peninsulas, the Mackinac Bridge has endured plenty. The structure is ready for more—lots more. The bridge is perhaps the most photographed feature of the state's icons and has as many faces and moods as there are angles of sun, moon, and weather. People drive from long distances to see it and enjoy the clean water-washed air of the Straits Area and its beaches, forests, and attractions. The Mackinac Bridge has opened the state of Michigan's highway system for commerce, travel, and tourism.

The Mackinac Bridge began celebrating the first year it was open by offering the public a chance to walk across the span. The event started as a race-walking activity, but soon became popular with thousands who wanted to return the following year and bring their friends. The Mackinac Bridge Walk today averages 50,000 to 60,000 participants and has become a Michigan Labor Day tradition. Weather can make the day a glorious adventure, or turn it into a cold soggy ordeal; remarkably there have been few Labor Days that have been so miserable that the walk has been curtailed in any way. Weather in the straits at that time of year has proven to usually be delightful. None of the Mackinac Bridge Walks have ever been completely canceled, rain or shine, in the first 50 years of participation.

Over the years, many different types of groups have arranged with the Mackinac Bridge Authority to cross as a group. It is fun and exciting, and crossing the bridge together provides an exhilarating activity that each group's members will never forget. Bicycle tours have enjoyed the crossing, as have parades of Harley Davidson motorcycles, Chevrolet Corvettes, motorcycle rallies, and participants in antique automobile and truck shows. The bicycle groups that cross normally do so at an early hour of the morning and are usually finished before many people realize they were on the bridge. The Corvette Crossroads is held in Mackinaw City in August and draws plenty of attention with its evening crossing, held with usually cooperative warm weather and convertible tops down. The Mackinac Bridge Authority is pleased to host the parade groups and strives to allow the events to take place in a safe, organized atmosphere. A permit is necessary in advance to secure permission to cross the bridge in this manner. (Above, courtesy of Jim Tamlyn; below, courtesy of Mackinaw Area Visitors Bureau.)

Winter blizzards, summer thunderstorms, and infamous "gales of November" have all tested the Mackinac Bridge without serious effects. The bridge has been struck by lightning several times and has survived without incident. On May 9, 2003, the highest wind speed ever recorded on the bridge occurred at 4:08 p.m. The anemometer read 124 miles per hour. Closures of the bridge have only amounted to about 50 in the first 50 years of the bridge's existence. Many more of those have come in recent years due to safety and liability concerns. High-profile vehicles such as campers and trucks are now routinely escorted across when winds reach 20 miles per hour, and all traffic is slowed and escorted when wind gauges reach 35 miles per hour. Complete closures have also taken place when ice falls from cables or bridge towers during spring thaws.

Completion of the Mackinac Bridge meant the junction of more than two Michigan peninsulas, for the bridge became a vital link in the Interstate Highway System as part of I-75. An addition to the St. Ignace interchange was the continuation of a four-lane concrete ribbon north to Sault Ste. Marie and the United States border with Canada. The connection now facilitates international commerce after being coupled with the International Bridge in later years. The bridge can handle 60,000 vehicles in a 24-hour period and averages about 12,000 per day. Building supplies, fuel, food supplies, automobile transports, and many other cargoes safely cross each day.

Security has increased on the bridge in recent years, with electric message signs installed at both approaches to the span capable of warning motorists of current conditions at the straits including wind speeds, road conditions, and fog. Strobe lights were placed at the 45 mile per hour posted speed limit signs just before the water's edge, making them more visible. Radio broadcasts on two different frequencies are available to be picked up on car radios with safety information. Patrols of the five-mile span have increased since St. Ignace Post No. 83 of the Michigan State Police opened just steps away from the tollbooth plaza at the north end of the bridge. (Courtesy of the Mackinaw City Chamber of Commerce.)

Fog can create low-visibility conditions on the bridge, but motorists are being protected in a variety of ways thanks to recent improvements in bridge security. A project to completely sandblast and repaint the entire bridge resulted in several moveable work platforms being installed under the bridge's road deck several years ago. Workmen can move from one spot to another under the suspended portion of the bridge on the motorized platforms, which travel along a set of I beam rails affording a view of the superstructure's underside. More recently, video cameras have been installed throughout the entire length of the bridge, viewable on computer screens in the Mackinac Bridge Authority's offices in St. Ignace. Bridge administrators and state police spokesmen will not say what additional measures may be in place due to possible terrorist threats. (Courtesy of the Mackinaw Area Visitors Bureau.)

The Mackinac Bridge is viewable and may be photographed from a variety of locations on the shores of either peninsula. A new, eight-acre Bridge View Park was dedicated on June 12, 2002, west of the toll plaza in Moran Township. The new park includes paved access roads, a walking path, picnic areas, trees, and landscaped areas containing flowers and shrubs. The observation building has five window sections facing the Straits of Mackinac and two entry doors. The back portion of the building has two restrooms. The bridge viewing area has been a popular place for people to visit and enjoy the Mackinac Bridge. The park provides a beautiful setting for the public to experience the spectacular view of the Mackinac Bridge and the Straits Area. The observation building is open from 8:00 a.m. until 9:00 p.m. daily. On the Mackinaw City side, public parks line the shores near the Old Mackinac Point Lighthouse, giving access to the water and a fabulous view of the bridge from the south. Seasonal restroom facilities are available with sidewalks, drinking fountains, and picnic areas. (Courtesy of the Mackinaw City Chamber of Commerce.)

On October 31, 2006, the Mackinac Bridge Authority and the Michigan Department of Transportation announced the release of the official 50th anniversary logo commemorating the opening of the Mackinac Bridge. The logo, seen here, is used with permission of the Mackinac Bridge Authority. The bridge celebrated 50 years of service in 2007 after first opening to traffic on November 1, 1957. The Mackinac Bridge Authority Board also approved special celebrations for July and November 2007, focused on the 50-year milestone along with plans for parades, honorary ceremonies, demonstrations by iron workers, live history presentations, photograph displays, musical entertainment, fireworks, release of a commemorative medallion, and other Straits-area community events. Indeed Michigan's greatest symbol deserved plenty of fanfare and honors. The bridge that Dr. David B. Steinman at first said would last 1,000 years, then amended his statement to say that he had miscalculated, "the Mackinac Bridge will still be standing after the pyramids of Egypt have fallen," had weathered its first 50 years in glorious fashion.

Visit us at
arcadiapublishing.com

Printed in the USA
CPSIA information can be obtained
at www.ICGtesting.com
LVHW071100071223
PP17991700003B/29